Healing Crystals
A Guide to Working with Carnelian

Brenda Hunt

copyright © Brenda Hunt 2013
All rights reserved world wide
No part of 'Healing Crystals - A Guide to Working with
Carnelian' may be reproduced or stored by any means
without the express permission of Brenda Hunt

Whilst reasonable care is taken to ensure the accuracy
of the information in this publication, no responsibility can
be accepted for the consequences of any actions based on
any opinions, information or advice found in the publication.

Healing information contained in this publication should
not be taken as a substitute for professional medical advice.
You should always consult your doctor on serious matters.

ISBN-13: 978-1482023527
ISBN-10: 1482023520

Contents

Introduction..4

    What is crystal healing?.................................4

Carnelian - the Friendly One 6

Carnelian in history...8

Choosing your Carnelian 10

    What form of crystal should you choose?.................11

How do you work with Carnelian?.....................13

Creating an elixir...15

    Working with an elixir. 16
    Elixir cream...16
    Elixir spray 17

Healing energies of Carnelian 18

    Spiritual healing.......................................19
    Mental and emotional healing 19
    Physical healing 20

Chakra healing 23

    The Sacral Chakra (2nd).........................24

Carnelian in jewellery. 28

Personal healing patterns 30

    Colour healing..32
    Healing your environment......................33

Cleansing crystals...34

    Moon Magic 37

About the Author..38

Introduction

This report has been written to introduce you to working with the healing energies of the beautiful gemstone carnelian, but of course you do also need some more general information about working with healing crystals, especially if this is one of your first crystals.

What is crystal healing?

When we talk about crystals in crystal healing we are talking about semiprecious gemstones rather than the  manmade glass crystals that are often used in jewellery and ornaments. The crystals that we use for their healing energies are the crystalline forms of minerals, and most of them are beautiful.

You will be familiar with many of them from the world of jewellery. Citrine, rock crystal or clear quartz, sapphire, emerald, tourmaline, tigers, eye, rose quartz, peridot, garnet and of course, Carnelian

All of these gemstones and many more have different healing energies that can help balance your energy field and help to heal you.

They work on different layers of our energy field - the spiritual, the emotional, the mental and the physical. You can work with single crystals or with many at the same time.

You can set aside time to create healing layouts or you can simply wear or carry them with you every day.

Healing crystals can be used by anyone in almost any situation. You can even work with healing crystals to help your pets and animals. I work with rose quartz to help rescue animals regain their confidence and trust of humans.

Although the idea of working with crystals for their healing properties may sound strange, in fact we work with the energy of crystals every day without even thinking about it. The quartz movement in your watch is a paper thin piece of quartz, which vibrates in response to an electric charge from the battery and allows the watch to keep good time.

This Piezoelectric property in quartz has been crucial to many of our technological advancements, not only watches but the computer chip, lasers, communication systems, ultrasound, and our entertainment systems are based on the quartz crystal.

We are happy to work with the healing energies of metals and crystals when it is approved of by science and the establishment. For instance, the antimicrobial and antibacterial properties of silver means that it is often impregnated into bandages and plasters.

Although this report will give you some general information about crystal healing, in the main it is specifically about the healing energies of the beautiful orange gemstone Carnelian.

It is one of a series of reports, each one of which focuses on a specific crystal or crystal family.

Carnelian - the Friendly One

Chemical formula: SiO_2 + (Fe,O,OH)
Crystal system: Trigonal
Mohs scale: hardness 6.5
Mineral group: oxide, quartz group
Colour: orange, red, yellow and brown
Sources: India, Peru, Britain, Iceland, Czech Republic, Romania and Slovakia
Chakra: sacral, root
Zodiac: Virgo, Leo Aries Cancer   Birthstone for July

Carnelian -traditionally called cornelian - is a form of chalcedony containing iron oxides, which cause the red tints in this beautiful gemstone.

In the past, it was often called Sard and the red brown form of carnelian is still often referred to as Sard. You also find it spelt cornelian, especially when jewellery or ancient carvings are being described.

It is a very common crystal and can be found in many parts of the world, although the best carnelian is found in India. The fact that it is easy to find makes it very reasonably priced and it's easy to find pieces to work with.

As it is one of the most generally useful crystals in the crystal healers toolkit, you should try to include a few pieces of it in your healing collection.

Choose some smooth tumbled pieces and some natural unpolished pieces so that you can use them in different situations.

Carnelian in history

Carnelian has a very long history with mankind and was one of the most coveted gems of antiquity, some of the oldest jewellery discovered features Carnelian.

It has been recovered from Bronze Age Minoan sites at Knossos, Crete showing its use in decorative arts dating from approximately 1800 BC.

The Minoan craftsmen were highly skilled in working with Carnelian or cornelian as it is more traditionally known. They carved beautifully intricate designs into the gemstone, creating seals that could be used to confirm ownership and the identity of boxes, jars or documents.

These seals were vital to the administration of the Minoan system, controlling the movement of goods and payments and confirming ownership of items. The beautiful carvings made each seal unique and easy to identify.

Carnelian has been an important gem in nearly every great civilisation in history, from the royalty of Ur (the pre-biblical Mesopotamian capital) to Napoleon, who brought a huge octagonal Carnelian back from Egypt with him after his campaign.

It also has a strong religious history.

Tomb offerings in Egypt show how the Egyptian goddess Isis used Carnelian to protect the dead on a journey through the afterlife. It is mentioned in the Bible, as one of the 'stones of fire' given to Moses for the breast plate of the high priest and it is the symbol of the Apostle Philip.

It was said to have been worn by Muhammad in a silver ring as his personal seal and it has always been held in high regard in the Muslim world.

It was also used widely during Roman times to make engraved gems for signet or seal rings, as hot wax does not stick to Carnelian. It was also highly valued and used in rings and signets by the Greeks, some of the intaglios (a gem carved in the negative relief) have retained their high polish better than many harder stones. The Romans associated dark Carnelian with men and paler Carnelian with women.

Sard, normally considered to be a darker form of carnelian, was used for Assyrian cylinder seals, Egyptian and Phoenician scarabs, and early Greek and Etruscan gems.

Tibetans created amulets of carnelian with turquoise and lapis lazuli which is considered to be a very protective combination.

In astrology Carnelian is considered the birthstone Virgo, while Hindu astrologers considered a secondary stone for Aries Scorpio. It is also one of the birthstones for July.

Choosing your Carnelian

You read a lot about choosing healing crystals, some of it makes it sound very complicated.

Many books and people will talk about the way that the crystal chooses you, which can make it sound as if you have to wait around until a crystal leaps out at you shouting "choose me, choose me". They will also talk about having to choose a crystal that has the right energy for you.

Of course both of these ideas are true, but it can sound very daunting to anyone who is new to crystal healing.

In fact, there is nothing complicated about it at all.

You will find that you are simply attracted to the right crystal. It will capture your attention, because it looks pretty or it's a lovely colour or a comforting shape, it will just catch your eye. And as far as having the right energy, it will simply feel right, feel comfortable in your hand. Sometimes you just won't want to put it down again in the shop - when that happens, you know it's the right crystal for you.

But you don't actually have to pick a crystal up to know it's the right one. You don't even have to be in the same room as it, or the same country for that matter. One of my own personal favourite crystals, a piece that I work with all the time, came to me from the other side of the world. It was on a website, not even a healing website, a gemstone one for the jewellery trade, and as soon as I saw the photo, I knew it was a crystal for me.

You also have to take into account where you are buying a crystal from. A lot of shops and websites sell crystals purely as a product, without any knowledge of their healing energies apart from the leaflets that they come with. You may still find a crystal that calls to you in a gift shop, but you will normally find it easier to find crystals with clean, clear energy if you deal with specialists who understand the crystals, their healing energies and how to work with them.

Don't be afraid to buy online. As long as you feel comfortable with the website and the people you are buying from, the right crystals tend to find their way to you.

What form of crystal should you choose?

You can choose your crystals in their natural unpolished form or polished (tumbled). You can choose small pieces (less than 1 inch across) to keep close to you in some way, or large pieces to place  somewhere in your room, or you can choose them as jewellery or carvings, keyrings, paperweights, healing wands or dowsing pendulums

There is no right or wrong type.

It depends entirely on how you want to work with them and what suits you.

The only thing that is wrong is choosing a piece of healing crystal purely on someone else's advice, a piece that you don't really feel comfortable with. Once you get it home you'll find that you don't actually work with it. It will sit on a shelf, or worse still, in a drawer, hidden from sight and mind.

For instance, you might buy a piece of jewellery that you're not comfortable with. A style that deep in your heart, you know you won't be comfortable wearing. There's no point in buying a large statement pendant when you always wear dainty jewellery. You might wear it for a few days, but eventually you will revert to your preferred style of jewellery and the beautiful but too large designer piece will sit in your jewellery box. The same thing will happen with any piece that doesn't suit your personal choice and style.

Is bigger better?

Will a great big heavy chunk of carnelian do you more good than a small delicate piece?

No.

When a crystal is inside your energy field, the actual size of it doesn't matter, so it isn't a case of more is more. A simple pair of carnelian ear studs or a small tumbled stone in your pocket will work as well as a large bead necklace or a large natural piece of carnelian on your desk in front of you.

As long as it is close to you the size won't affect the energy you feel.

The exception to this is when you want the carnelian to improve the energy of a larger space, a room or work area. If the crystal needs to energise a larger area, or you want to keep a piece further away from you – somewhere in the room or in your work area, but not within arm's length – then you will need a larger piece so that it has enough energy to fill a larger area. Choose a large natural piece at least 4" (10cm) across.

The golden rule in choosing your crystal is to make sure that you like it.

So when you're choosing your carnelian, or any crystal, trust your instincts.

In fact, that's one of the most important lessons in working with crystals - learn to trust your instincts and carnelian can help you develop this ability, giving you to confidence to trust your `gut' reaction

How do you work with Carnelian?

There is nothing magical about working with carnelian or indeed any healing crystal.

You don't have to do anything to them, you don't have to buy crystals that have been specially treated, had spells cast over them, been infused with Reiki energy or anything else beyond your own personal ability to choose and work with the right crystals.

You are working with the energy of the crystal itself. They are the crystalline forms of the minerals that we need for health, and that we get through the food chain from the earth - although of course you should never eat the actual crystal.

For instance malachite contains copper, howlite includes calcium, carnelian contains iron and the piezoelectric property of quartz has been used by industry and technology for many years. It is involved in the huge variety of everyday items such as the gas lighter, quartz watch, the autofocus on your camera and of course the silicon chip, powering almost everything we use nowadays.

So, as a general rule you really just need to have your choice of crystal close to you, inside your own electromagnetic field, about arm's-length around you. A good guide is your feeling of what is 'your space' when someone gets too physically close to you.

The crystal doesn't actually need to touch your skin, although there is nothing wrong with this with most crystals and carnelian is one of the crystals where it actually can be more effective if it is in contact with your skin.

There are some crystals that are toxic such as unpolished malachite, and you should take care with these crystals, not keeping them in contact with the skin.

Most of the crystals you will actually come across are perfectly safe. A good crystal book will give you information about the crystals you should take care with.

Carnelian is safe in any of its forms - natural, polished or carved, as cabochons or beads set into jewellery.

You can buy some crystal items that are designed to be touched, such as palm stones which are flat, smooth, polished pieces of crystal, often with a groove on the surface to rub your thumb against.

Working with a Carnelian palm stone is a very gentle energy, very calming and soothing and is excellent for anyone who is feeling low or sad. Just holding a Carnelian palm stone is very soothing as the very action of playing with a polished item, whether it is gemstone or coin is very calming and when you work with the crystal palm stone, you are also working with the energy of that specific crystal.

The way you work with your carnelian will depend to a certain extent on the size and style that you have chosen.

Obviously, if you have chosen a piece of jewellery you will wear it. A tumbled stone or palm stone will probably be in your pocket and a large piece of carnelian will be on a desk or an ornament in your living room.

Carnelian is one of those gemstones that you will probably have in various different forms, because it is so useful and because it is a beautiful natural gemstone that lends itself to many different forms and styles.

Creating an elixir

Although you'll work with the actual crystal in most forms of crystal healing and Carnelian is no exception, there

are times when it can be useful to create an elixir of the gemstone.

An elixir is a useful way to work with the energy of the healing crystal in situations where you may prefer not to use an actual gemstone, such as working with animals or young children.

You must take care when making an elixir. Some crystals can be destroyed by water and a few are toxic and must only be made using a special method that does not allow physical contact between the crystal and the water.

Carnelian is an excellent crystal for an elixir, it is safe to use, and it will not be damaged by the water.

Making a general elixir is simple. Place your carnelian – a polished tumbled stone is best - into a clear glass container of purified or spring water. You can also use distilled water, which does not contain any energy signature of its own.

It's important to use a clear container as a coloured glass container would affect the elixir, adding colour energy to it.

Place the glass or jug in the sunlight for about three hours during the early morning, or in moonlight overnight. It's best to cover the container with a piece of white muslin or kitchen towel to keep your elixir clean.

Remove the carnelian before you use the elixir. The energy of the carnelian has been infused into the elixir and you don't want to risk anyone swallowing the actual crystal!

When you use an elixir, you are 'filling' yourself with the energy of the Carnelian, and it can be very powerful. So you should always start by drinking small doses throughout the day, rather than a single full glass. The elixir is absorbed faster the more the body needs the energy.

I prefer to make the elixir and use it fresh but if you do want to store it for a few days make sure that you keep it in a cool dark place and away from any strong energies.

Working with an elixir.

Once you've made your elixir, you can of course simply drink it, but there are other ways of working with any gem Elixir.

- Add a few drops to a plain massage oil.
- Rub a few drops onto your hands, then hold them in front of your nose and inhale deeply.
- Massage drops onto your temple before meditating.
- Add a few drops to your bathwater.
- Put a few drops in your washing machine.

Elixir cream

You can also add the elixir to a body cream. Find an un-perfumed cream as pure from additives as you can, and mix a few drops of your elixir into a small pot of this cream.

It is then best to keep the cream in a cool area, possibly the fridge. You can then use this to ease pain or tension by rubbing the cream onto the affected area.

A elixir cream of carnelian is particularly useful for easing muscle and joint aches and pains, whether a temporary muscle injury or the pain of arthritis.

Only make enough Elixir cream for a few weeks. It's best to keep it fresh.

Elixir spray

You can also use a gem Elixir as a spray using a small plant spray bottle such as you get in the garden centres, or possibly a perfume atomiser.

Fill the bottle with purified or spring water and add a few drops of the elixir to it. Once it's made you should keep in the fridge.

You can use an elixir spray to treat a room, simply spraying the air as you would with an air freshener. You can also use it as a treat for your plants to improve their health.

An elixir spray can be used as an aura spray in a child's room or for a pet. This is a very safe way to introduce crystal healing without the risk of an actual crystal being swallowed.

A Carnelian elixir spray can be very helpful to ease the pain of an elderly beloved pet, whose joints aren't quite what they used to be. Put some on your hands and then rub your pet gently, or use the spray either around the animal or around its sleep area or favourite spot.

Healing energies of Carnelian

Carnelian is a very powerful crystal for healing, with a very high energy and should be in anyone's collection of healing crystals. You will find that Carnelian will be a gemstone that you reach for regularly and will fast become one of your favourite healing energies.

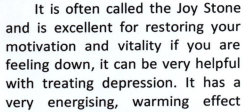

It is often called the Joy Stone and is excellent for restoring your motivation and vitality if you are feeling down, it can be very helpful with treating depression. It has a very energising, warming effect which can be very invigorating if you are feeling sluggish or lethargic, this makes a lovely crystal to wear regularly during the winter if you are affected by the cold weather and a lack of sunshine.

It has also been used since Egyptian times to remove lethargy and depression and bring joy, making it a wonderful crystal if your vitality or energy is reduced, especially after recovering from illness, as it can also help the connective tissues and with wound healing, it is a lovely crystal for someone recovering from an operation.

Carnelian is also a very protective crystal, giving you a warm feeling of being sheltered from negative energies. It can help strengthen your courage and help you make positive decisions when you're facing choices in life. It's also a very good energy when you are lacking motivation or feeling apathetic about life, unable to make choices or even face the choices.

Spiritual healing.

Carnelian has long been known as a crystal of great spirituality. It is believed to be very protective as you journey from one life to the next, allowing you to accept the cycle of life, calming fears about death. In Egypt, it was used as protection for the journey to the afterlife.

It can be used to strengthen the spirit giving you the courage to stand up for what you believe in, to be idealistic, and to work for a good cause in the face of adversity.

This spiritual courage can allow you to take a positive attitude in making your life choices. It can help you overcome indecision or procrastination, strengthening your spirit so that you take the action that is required, rather than waiting for something to just happen to improve your life.

This spiritual energy can give you a sense of security and allow you to believe in your own power and your own talents and giving you the strength and courage to make positive life choices and embrace your dreams.

Wearing a Carnelian regularly, even permanently, will help you make the most of this spiritual energy. It should be worn in contact with the skin.

Mental and emotional healing

Carnelian is considered to aid and balance creativity, and to improve your concentration, which can make it very useful when you are working on a project, whether that is writing a book or redecorating room.

It can also help lift your spirits in dealing with your emotional life and give you the kind of courage that gets you through every day life, overcoming problems and pitfalls.

Carnelian is a very useful crystal to choose when you need to solve problems. It helps you remain logical and pragmatic, concentrating on what can be done, rather than daydreaming about what might be done.

It helps you overcome negative thinking, allowing you to trust yourself and your own ideas, but far from being a limiting energy, it can help you focus and turn daydreams into reality, by helping you concentrate on getting the job done.

It's a very powerful energy when you are feeling confused or overwhelmed, because it can help to stabilise your energy and anchor you in the present rather than constantly worrying about what has happened in the past or what might happen in the future.

It is a very helpful energy for meditation, because it allows you to focus and improves concentration.

Carnelian is a wonderful energy for difficult relationships. It can help protect you against resentment, envy or even rage, whether from yourself or from others. It can allow you to trust yourself and help you overcome any kind of abuse, either in the present or in the past, even pain that you are carrying from past lives. It is considered to help you deal with jealousy or possessiveness in relationships and can also help with sexual problems or anxieties such as frigidity or impotence

Physical healing

Physically, Carnelian is believed to help stimulate the absorption of nutrients, minerals and vitamins, which can help improve the quality of the blood and circulation, ensuring a good blood supply to the organs and tissues which of course has beneficial effects on the entire body, helping with tissue regeneration and improving the metabolism (converting food into energy).

Carnelian can also be used when dealing with problems with the kidneys.

It is considered to help with respiratory problems such as asthma and allergies or any problems with breathing, whether it is helping ease a long term, chronic problem or helping you get through a summer cold or blocked sinuses.

It has also been used to help ease menstrual cramps and by helping balance the lower chakras, it can help improve fertility and help with problems in the reproductive organs. It has been used to help treat impotence.

It has also been used to help alleviate rheumatism and arthritis, one of the most popular uses of Carnelian in modern life (along with its ability to ease asthma and allergies). Either wear a piece of jewellery, carry a piece in your pocket or place a piece where it will be close to you for extended periods of time. For instance, at the chair where you sit or under your pillow as you sleep

It can also help to bring relief to pulled muscles, whether from over doing the housework or from intense exercise. There are many ways in which you can pull a muscle and all of them lead to the same kind of pain. Anything that can reduce that and reduce the length of the injury is welcome. Simply place a piece of Carnelian onto the injury until the pain eases. You may just require a few minutes of holding the Carnelian in place or you might prefer to bandage it over the injury and leave in place overnight.

Carnelian can also help ease problems of the lower back and is considered to speed the healing of broken bones, strained muscles and torn ligaments. An elixir cream or aura spray can be applied to the injury or painful area as often as is required. An elixir can also help heal cuts and scratches.

Placing a circle of Carnelian around you as you relax or meditate can be very calming and life affirming. It is a good technique if you are feeling overwhelmed by a problem or stressed in general.

Chakra healing

Ancient Indian Sanskrit texts teach us of the Chakra system. They tell of centres of energy in the human body, with seven major points arranged along the line of the spine.

During our daily life, they can become unbalanced, which can hinder the flow of energy throughout the body. Over time this can contribute to illness or emotional upset.

We are very complex systems, and many illnesses cannot be treated simply. All parts of our body interact with others and we should treat ourselves as a whole rather than as a collection of parts.

Keeping our energy system in balance is a vital part of maintaining our general well-being.

In Eastern Yogic texts, the chakras are visualised as lotus flowers, with the petals and fine roots of the flower distributing the life force – or Prana – throughout the physical body and converting the energy into chemical, hormonal and cellular changes.

The vibration of crystals can harmonise the Chakras and allow the energy to flow freely again, which is why it can be helpful to use a charka healing layout as well as the more direct use of a crystal or crystals that are specifically linked to the problem or illness that you want to treat.

Different crystals and colour, and the vibrational energy of the colour are linked to each charka, and for this type of healing, the colour is an important part of the choice that you make.

The Sacral Chakra (2nd)

Svadhisthana – Sva = vital force: adhisthana = seat or abode

Also known as the water chakra or sweetness. 'In your own dwelling place'

Located 1" below the navel. and above the genitals.

This balances sexuality, emotion, desire, creativity, intuition and self worth. If it is blocked you may feel emotionally explosive, lacking energy, have feelings of isolation. Physically it can lead to kidney and uterine disorders, lower back pain, impotence and prostate problems

- Gland: ovaries/testes
- Sense: taste
- Colour orange
- Intake: fluids
- Element: water
- Oils: rose; jasmine, sandalwood
- Symbol: 6 petal orange-red lotus flower containing 2nd lotus flower and an upward pointing crescent moon
- Feminine - Yin

Areas of effect

This chakra is connected with sexual energy, affecting attraction, emotion, vitality, desire, creativity, intuition, self worth, sexuality, the reproductive system and all fluid functions of the body - that is, the bladder and kidneys, prostate, lymphatic system, fat deposits and skin.

Balanced

The sacral chakra is a spiritual centre. When it is balanced and activated you will have vitality and health will flow. You have good self esteem, a sense of direction, emotional stability and a healthy relationship to desire, pleasure and intimacy.

You are able to trust, to be expressive. You are attuned to your feelings and emotions and are able to see the positive side of situations.

The balance of the Sacral chakra allows you to find pleasure in life, approaching things with enthusiasm, being willing to enjoy life and concentrate on the positive aspects of existence.

People with a balanced Sacral chakra are often seen as 'lucky', but it is just that they tend to see the good in situations rather than the negatives.

Imbalance

Imbalance can manifest as impotence, frigidity or an addiction to sex, emotional immaturity, a tendency to jealousy, fear of intimacy, guilt and obsession. You may feel emotionally explosive, lacking energy or have feelings of isolation.

Physically it can lead to kidney and uterine disorders, IBS, lower or middle back pain, impotence and prostate problems, infertility

The sacral charka – Ovaries/testes

Each chakra corresponds to part of the glandular system. The sacral chakra corresponds to the ovaries & testes.

These are the glands that produce the hormones that control such things as body hair and depth of voice as well as reproduction.

The ovaries (female) produce Progesterone and Oestrogen (a mainly female hormone). They are important for the health of the reproductive tissues, breasts, skin and brain. Too much can lead to fluid retention, weight gain, migraines and more seriously - over stimulation of breasts, ovaries and uterus, which can lead to cancer.

Too little of the hormone can lead to hot flushes, vaginal dryness, rapid skin ageing and excessive bone loss. It has also been linked to dementia.

Excess oestrogen in relation to testosterone in men, is thought to lead to prostate problems.

The testes (male) produce the male sex hormones, mainly testosterone, which has an effect on the growth of muscle mass and strength, increased bone density, growth and strength. It is also the hormone that deepens the voice and affects the growth of the beard.

Carnelian is an excellent crystal to help keep the sacral chakra in balance, but in general you should work on keeping your whole Chakra system in balance rather than just concentrating on a single chakra

Carnelian in jewellery.

In the past Carnelian was a regular choice for jewellery, whether worn as protective amulets, in a ring as an important seal, as beautiful beads or as protection in this life or in the afterlife.

It was one of the favoured gems in both the Egypt and Tibet, often combined with lapis lazuli and turquoise.

Today, you are more likely to find Carnelian jewellery that Is created by an Artisan, rather than mass produced in an jewellery shop. The beautiful and rich orange shades of Carnelian make it perfect for jewellery and combines well with either silver or gold.

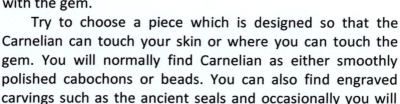

As Carnelian works best if used over a long period, jewellery is an easy way to work with the gem.

Try to choose a piece which is designed so that the Carnelian can touch your skin or where you can touch the gem. You will normally find Carnelian as either smoothly polished cabochons or beads. You can also find engraved carvings such as the ancient seals and occasionally you will find it faceted, which allows the light to bounce off it at different angles although it is an opaque gem rather than a translucent gemstone such as citrine or amethyst

You can wear it in many ways, as polished beads, a pendant, earrings or bracelet, cufflinks, in a belt

Working with Carnelian

buckle or as a ring - it makes a very good signet ring and it's a very unisex gemstone which has traditionally been worn by men as well as women. In fact in ancient societies, where it was often carved as a seal, it was more often worn by men.

Whichever style or type of jewellery you choose, try to pick a design that you will be comfortable with, and therefore will wear on a regular basis to absorb the energy of the gemstone. If you prefer variety in your jewellery, you could choose to have a collection of different designs. But once you start working with carnelian, most people find that they want to have a gemstone close to them most of the time.

Personal healing patterns

As with any healing crystal, the carnelian crystal must be inside your own energy field (about arms length) in order to be able to work on balancing you.

That is why it is easy to wear your carnelian set into jewellery, to carry a piece in your pocket or keep it under your pillow.

But you can also place the carnelian either on you or around you when you want to spend time actually concentrating on healing and balancing your energy.

A healing pattern of natural Clear Quartz points surrounding the body, with a carnelian polished stone placed on the sacral chakra can be an extremely powerful healing pattern.

This general healing pattern can be used with many different crystals actually placed on the body – either a single crystal for a very specific healing energy or a range of crystals creating a healing recipe.

The general healing pattern of quartz points works because of the ability of natural quartz points to direct energy, either negative energy out of your energy field or positive energy into your energy field. The energy flows in the direction of the natural point.

Find a time and place where you can relax and will be undisturbed, ideally for about 20 minutes.

Make sure that the energy you will be directing into your energy field is fresh and pure, don't set up next to the

Working with Carnelian

TV, computer or close to electricity pylons. Wear comfortable clothing - you don't want to be distracted by an irritatingly tight waistband!

You might want to light some aromatherapy candles or play some gentle music to help create a bubble of relaxations and peace,

Place the points facing away from the body to draw negative energy away – leave for about 5 minutes.

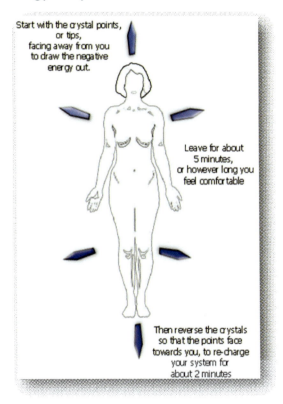

Start with the crystal points, or tips, facing away from you to draw the negative energy out.

Leave for about 5 minutes, or however long you feel comfortable

Then reverse the crystals so that the points face towards you, to re-charge your system for about 2 minutes

Then reverse the points to face in towards the body for about 2 minutes, to draw fresh positive energy into the energy field.

31

Remove the crystals and relax, allowing your energy field to absorb the fresh healing energy.

Carnelian can also be laid on the body for healing, placing it either directly on or in the general area of the part of the body that requires healing. For chakra healing, this would be on the sacral chakra, just below the navel.

For breathing problems, you can relax with the carnelian on the third eye chakra, at the top of the nose, just between the eyes, to ease sinus pain. You can also place it on your chest to ease breathing difficulties, or wherever you 'feel' is the right position.

For aches and pains, whether arthritis and general pain, or a specific injury, place the carnelian at the point of the pain.

Forming a healing circle of carnelian gems is also a very calming healing pattern and works well with meditation. Simply select your crystals and place them in a circle surrounding you. Carnelian is a very gentle healer so you can work with it for as long as you feel comfortable.

Carnelian can be very helpful for easing the pain of menstrual cramps, simply hold a piece of carnelian against your skin until the pain eases.

Colour healing

It's well accepted that colours can affect us. How we feel, our moods, our emotional state – either positive or negative. The colours we choose for our clothes, our rooms, our accessories and our jewellery can have a profound effect on how we feel and we often chose a colour subconsciously, depending on how we feel at the time.

Orange is created by mixing red and yellow. It's next to red on the electromagnetic spectrum and like red, is still as warm and stimulating colour. It's the colour of joy and vitality, very useful for lifting moods and bringing relief from depression.

In colour healing, orange can be used as a general tonic and has been found to be helpful for arthritis, muscle cramps and for the general health of the kidneys.

Carnelian is a wonderful way to introduce the healing energies of orange into your life. Not everyone is brave enough to wear such a beautiful vivid colour on a larger scale.

Healing your environment

Crystals can be used to 'heal' your environment as well as your health and emotions. Not only do they create a beautiful decorative focus for a room, they can actively help to reduce the effects of emotional stress.

In general, it is better to use pieces of rough, unpolished crystals rather than tumbled crystals for environmental use as they will spread their effect further - throughout the room rather than just within your own personal aura. In this case, larger pieces will have a 'larger' effect, as their radius of influence will be wider. Although a bowl of small tumbled carnelian can help create sense of safety and security in a room

When you want to cleanse the energy in a larger area, you have to work with larger crystals that can spread their energies further.

Carnelian is considered to be a very protective energy, and pieces of carnelian placed around the entrance to your home can help create a stable, balanced energy, drawing in positive energy and good luck into your life.

Cleansing crystals

A new crystal should always be cleansed before you use it for healing. This is not actually to clean dirt from it, but the unwanted energy it will have gathered from other people.

You should also cleanse your crystals between specific healing sessions to avoid transferring negative energies and you should cleanse them as a general habit when you feel that they are less affective or on a regular basis. Learn to trust your instincts, you will learn to feel when they need cleansing and recharging.

There are many ways suggested for cleansing but care should be taken before you decide on which method to use. Some crystals would be destroyed by water, while others would fade in sunlight - amethyst, rose quartz and aventurine can all be badly affected by too much sunlight.

Personally I prefer to avoid some of the other methods that are sometimes recommended.

Placing a crystal in salt water or sitting it directly in salt can be very damaging for some crystals. A salt solution, can penetrate some crystal structures, making the stone cloudy or discolouring it. Sitting some crystals in salt would destroyed them altogether. For instance, placing an Opal on a bed of salt would draw the water from it, changing it from an Opal gemstone into a much less valuable piece of chalcedony.

I also prefer to avoid burying a crystal. Apart from the obvious danger of not being able to find it again, there is the risk that the soil conditions will damage the crystal. For instance, your soil may be too acid.

In crystal healing, we are working with the energies of crystals and we should respect them and take care of the crystals we have chosen so that they will continue to work with us for many years.

An Amethyst bed or druze is a very useful crystal for helping to cleanse other crystals. Simply place your other crystals, gently onto the surface of the natural points and allow the Amethyst to focus the negative energy away from them. Leave them for approximately 3 to 4 hours. This  method is gentle enough for any of your crystals, even those set into jewellery although you do need to take care that soft gems will not be scratched by the amethyst, which is a hard crystal (7 on the MOHs scale).

Do not leave the crystals on the amethyst too long, as amethyst is very energising and other crystals can begin to take on the energy of the amethyst. If you do leave them too long, set your crystals aside to allow them to recover their own energy.

You can also use sea salt to cleanse the negative energy from your carnelian. You can find sea salt at most supermarkets.

Place the dry sea salt into a clear glass bowl. It is important to use clear glass as you do not want to introduce colour energy into the cleansing.

Sit a smaller clear glass bowl in the sea salt so that it is surrounded by the salt.

Place your carnelian (or other crystals) into the second bowl so that it is surrounded by but not touching the salt. Leave it for three to four hours.

You can reuse the salt for many months for cleansing, just cover it so that it doesn't get too dusty but never use it for cooking once you have been cleansing crystals, you don't want to ingest the negative energy.

If you're comfortable with dowsing with a pendulum you can cleanse your crystals in this way as well. Just ask your pendulum to remove the negative energy from your crystals and then hold it over the crystals and let it move as it wants until it comes naturally to a halt. This will make sense if you are an experienced dowser - if you've never worked with a pendulum - it'll make no sense at all!

You should cleanse your crystals when you 'feel' that they need it, there are no timetables for this. A crystal that absorbs negative energy - for instance snowflake obsidian or quartz crystal kept beside a TV - will require quite frequent cleansing. So will a crystal that you are using to absorb pain, such as malachite, which for severe pain should be cleansed daily. But you may feel that other crystals only need cleansing after a number of months, in fact, a citrine pendant worn every day, may only need cleansing every six months.

Use your intuition - you can tell when your crystal is no longer as effective as it was. Until you get the 'feel' for them, a good guideline is about once a month.

Moon Magic

Carnelian loves the energy of the moon and leaving it in the moonlight can be a very powerful cleanser. It can also be a powerful way of charging your crystal for a specific healing task.

The different phases of the moon have different spiritual energies.

The new moon is for new beginnings, starting new ventures. It's also the time that is recommended for jobhunting.

The waxing moon between the new and full moon is considered to be the energy of getting things done, such as dealing with matters of courage and luck, wealth or success.

The full moon is very cleansing and energising, perfect for clearing your crystals of unwanted energy once you have finished a healing task.

The waning moon between the full and new moon is a very good time to cleanse crystals if you have been working with them in dealing with a lot of negative energies such as serious illness, addictions or negative emotions, as it is a very good energy for banishing that negativity.

The dark of the moon, the three days before the new moon, is traditionally a time for recuperation, rest and meditation.

When you want to work with your crystals for a specific task, you can choose the right phase of the moon to suit the energy you require and charge your carnelian with that energy before you start your healing work.

About the Author

From a long line of healers on the West Coast of Ireland, Brenda has worked with healing crystals and a dowsing pendulum for almost 20 years and is a member of the British Society of Dowsers.

She regularly gives talks and classes on dowsing, vibrational therapies, crystal healing and colour healing as well as writing books, articles and well known series of Core Information charts on a number of alternative therapies.

you can contact her at: brenda@healing-earth.co.uk
website: www.healing earth.co.uk

If you have enjoyed this book, please give feedback at Amazon

Whilst reasonable care is taken to ensure the accuracy of the information in this publication, no responsibility can be accepted for the consequences of any actions based on any opinions, information or advice found in the publication.

Healing information contained in this publication should not be taken as a substitute for professional medical advice. You should always consult your doctor on serious matters.

Printed in Great Britain
by Amazon